DOMAIN OF ENTIRETY

PALMETTO
PUBLISHING
Charleston, SC
www.PalmettoPublishing.com

Domain Of Entirety
Copyright © 2023 by Bradley W. Witt, Sr.

All rights reserved
No portion of this book may be reproduced, stored in a retrieval system, or transmitted in any form by any means–electronic, mechanical, photocopy, recording, or other–except for brief quotations in printed reviews, without prior permission of the author.

First Edition

Paperback ISBN: 9798822918108
eBook ISBN: 9798318835391

DOMAIN OF ENTIRETY

BRADLEY W. WITT, SR.

CONTENTS

Preface vii
Introduction xi
   Section I: Love, Hate, and Karma xi
   Section II: Entirety xiv
   Section III: Free Will xviii
   Section IV: The Experience xix

Chapter 1: Origins 1
   The Infinite and Creator 1
   The Origin of Time 1
   Love—The Source: Love Is Not Its Name 3

Chapter 2: Measures and Communication 5
   The Concept of Shape 5
   Color 7
   Numbers 8
   Communication and Harmony 11

Chapter 3: Physical within the Metaphysical ... 13
   Point of Nothingness and Everything 13
   Metaphysical to Physical 14
   Body and Soul 15
   The Chakra System and Its Resonance
   with Densities and Universal Octaves 17
   Catalyst 26

    Continual Amnesia.......................... 28
    Multiple Realities........................... 31

Chapter 4: Positive and Negative.............. 34
    Positive and Negative........................ 34
    Good and Evil 36

Chapter 5: Rhythm, Frequency, and Synchronicity 38
    The Rhythm (Ebb and Flow)................. 38
    Density and Dimensions and the Electromagnetic Spectrum 39
    Densities Further Explained 39
    Resonance, Synchronicity, and Our Quantum Reality...................................... 41
    Bonus Section............................... 45
    Grids, Consciousness, and Akashic 45
    Time.. 47
    Is Source the Primordial Original Computer?.. 49
    The Womb of Source........................ 50
    Destiny and Fate 51

Closing 53

Bibliography 55

PREFACE

For most of my life, I was asleep, trapped in the dogmatic reality many humans on this phenomenal planet live in. I was raised by the Bible, and for a majority of my life, it was the Bible way or no way. The Bible is an important book of history and enlightenment, but in my opinion, it is greatly misinterpreted and misused. There are hundreds or even thousands of ancient texts, tablets, and oral traditions with just as much importance as the Bible. Most of my adult life was spent as an oxymoron—I read the Bible, prayed, attended church sporadically, drank heavily, smoked marijuana, smoked cigarettes, and experimented with other drugs. About three and a half years ago, while in the hospital for an abscess on my tonsil, I decided to sober up. I put down the alcohol and marijuana and never looked back.

Deep inside, I always knew there was more to reality than what meets the eye. While under the strong hold of Christianity, I still wondered how someone could be damned to eternal hellfire if they were born into sin against their will. As a child, I would draw pictures of souls leaving their bodies. One day, before I was spiritually woken, I had the thought cross my mind that once we die and leave these bodies, we are truly free. I felt that after my physical death, my soul could go travel the cosmos where I want to be. Little did I know at that time that it was Source communicating with me through my higher self. This was more than a thought; I truly felt this. Once I sobered up at the age of thirty-eight, the journey began.

Once sober, my interest in otherworldly subjects grew stronger. Even as a child, I always had a keen interest in *Star Wars*. It was more than an interest; it was a desire to be there. As sobriety took place, I became a serious Trekkie—my interest in life on other planets grew deeper. I started watching *UFO Chronicles* on Tubi. One thing led to another until I ran into Gaia television and subscribed, and I have been a huge fan ever since. As I dove further in, I started doing my own personal readings and research. *The Law Of One (Ra Material)*, *The Kybalion*, *Gnostic Gospels*, *Emerald Tablets*, and many more readings have fed my cravings.

After subscribing to Gaia television, I was opened up to meditation; I now meditate daily and have done so for over two years. Once I started meditating daily, I took on yoga. In actuality, meditation and yoga are one and the same. Meditation opened my mind to so much—it is a great tool for a recovering addict. From a person who experienced substance abuse, I can say from my personal experience that meditation is better than drugs and alcohol if done right.

Meditation opened my mind to the true reality about who we really are as multidimensional entities. With my mind's eye, I saw life on other planets. I now understand things in ways that I didn't before a meditation session; I would get downloads that would hit me out of nowhere within seconds. Now, I'm here to share my Source knowledge and newfound accelerated wisdom.

INTRODUCTION

Section I: Love, Hate, and Karma

There is resonance in love, knowledge, and wisdom. Love is the unconditional creative force. Knowledge is the gift of obtaining the functions of eternal Source. Source is entirety, so Source is all that exists. In actuality, each soul has Source knowledge, but our avatar bodies can process only tiny increments. As our souls advance their way up through higher avatar bodies in reincarnations, the bodies can hold more Source wisdom. Once a soul is back with Source, all functions of eternal Source will be obtained, for all will be one. When knowledge is applied to day-to-day living in a positive manner, this is wisdom. Knowledge must be obtained before wisdom, usually by oral traditions, readings, academia, and meditation. Outside of our incarnations, our higher self, which is our soul, has constant Source knowledge and wisdom. As aforementioned, once a soul is back with Source, functions of eternal Source are constant. Our physical bodies cut off our connection to Source knowledge.

There is resonance with prolonged hatred and foolishness—love and hate are on the same pole. They are polar opposites, like hot and cold or wisdom and foolishness. It is okay to briefly hate; an entity may hate a situation that could be detrimental to them—this brief hatred could be used to get out of the harmful situation. This is when Source knowledge should be applied. Once out of the situation, the entity should apply forgiveness, then the entity must go back to living in love. If hatred is prolonged, this will first lead to bad karma and foolish behavior. If an entity is living in hatred, he or she is on the polar opposite of love, and there is no resonance with wisdom. They will apply egotistical, spontaneous, and sometimes silly measures instead of knowledge—and this equates to foolishness.

Negative karma is built up desire for the soul to correct energies that have gone amok. What is this energy, and has it really gone amok? Many people think karma is "What goes around comes around." In actuality, what goes around and comes around is the law of attraction. Essentially, the law of attraction means that what energies we put out are also the energies we attract. Further into this book you'll learn that our vibrational frequencies are based on our mentality—so if a person does something physically bad or good to another, the vibration put out is based on the thought. The physical action was a thought before it came into fruition; thoughts produce and emit energy. The energy put out attracts similar energy—and this is the law of attraction, just as similar people attract one another, down to the molecular and quantum levels, as in "like attracts like." The law of attraction is based on daily events in a single incarnation, while karma is carried from one incarnation to the next. Negative karma is the notion that one has to correct a misdeed that they themselves have committed. In some cases, a soul will reincarnate to correct a negative karma, even though the primary purpose of reincarnation is for soul growth and evolution.

Now that we know what the energy is that we are trying to correct, has it really gone amok? The answer is yes and no. Source is conscious, and we are conscious beings. As conscious entities, we build our realities based on perception. If we perceive that we have a karmic debt, then it is so. If we would simply forgive ourselves during an incarnation, we could free ourselves from some negative karma—this is why forgiveness of self is primary and then follows the forgiveness of others so we don't hold on to any prolonged hatred. Prolonged hatred holds a low frequency, which can be a hindrance to a soul and would need karmic correcting.

Now a little about positive karma: Positive karma is just as real as negative karma but much simpler to deal with. If a person led a life of mostly positive karma, the entity will have a smooth and easy incarnation without a lot of kinks. Individuals who live in love and practice wisdom will have a light karmic load; light karmic load equals little karmic debt. As long as souls keep this process up during all incarnations—which souls normally do as they gain wisdom from each incarnation—they will have a faster rate of ascension back to oneness with Source.

Section II: Entirety
This book is a book about entirety. What is entirety? Entirety is all that exists; entirety is before and after time. All dimensions, densities, and realities in all of the multiverses are entirety—notice I said multiverses instead of multiverse. I believe we live in a conscious existence; we have to think much larger than the universe. In my view, "universe" is a minute term. One universe could be part of a system of universes that makes up the multiverse; there could then be an endless number of multiverses. You have to think huge when it comes to reality being conscious.

Many people are familiar with the term Source. Source is the consciousness that gives creation to all that exists. In this book, I will use the term Source very often. As aforementioned, I theorize that we live in a conscious existence—all that exists is mental. Essentially, all existence originated from a thought; possibly one single thought started it all.[1] That single thought then turned into eons of thoughts. Those eons of thoughts are the endless numbers of realities, probabilities, and possibilities.

In the beginning was the primordial thought—that thought was first, and every thought that exists in every single thinking soul derives from that thought. Researchers estimate that humans average 70,000 thoughts a day. If a single human averages 70,000 thoughts a day, imagine how many thoughts Source averages since before and after time as we know it—wrap your thoughts around that notion for a minute.

Every material object in our possession was a thought before it was produced. It is true that we think things into reality; the thought always comes first. Material objects of our creation don't just appear out of thin air—first there is the thought. The thought comes into fusion with planning; planning is the molding of the thought. The molded thought is then physically manifested with the use of our body, usually our hands—this is proof that we are creators. Our creativity is instinctively ingrained in us from Source. We are fractals of entirety; all of Source is us, and all of us is Source.

In our third density bodies, we cannot manifest just by thought alone—we have the thought first, then we

---

[1] Gary Bean(ED), Austin Bridges(ED), (2018), "The RA Contact: Teaching The Law Of One(Volume1)," L/L Research.

must use our physical bodies to manifest that thought into a physical object. Advanced fourth density beings and higher can manifest thoughts into creation at will. Fifth density entities and higher can even manifest what their physical appearance will be. We are all capable of doing this because we are all multidimensional beings. In this third density body we reside in, we have no clue of the power we possess—our existence right now is just one of the many existences our soul inhabits. Our soul possesses all of its incarnations at once; this is across all dimensions, realities, and timelines. Our soul is a fractal of Source—we are Source and we are the creator.

Each and every living quantum particle that exists in entirety is one—all existence is one Source. We are all one, distorted to seem as individuals. We all have a higher self and over soul. Our higher self is the multidimensional aspect of ourselves—we exist across all dimensions. This may be hard for most to grasp, but once we are out of these third density bodies, it will all make sense. This concept will be further explained in the next couple of paragraphs.

The first distortion of Source is the spirit. The spirit is the all-seeing, omnipresent soul of all existence across all realities, time periods, dimensions, densities, and multiverses; the spirit is the giver of life. Although the spirit is its own entity, it is still one with Source. The spirit divides itself into eons of fractals of itself—these fractals are our souls, or what I would call spirit fractals or mini spirits.

The soul, being a fractal of the main spirit, mimics spirit—although souls aren't omnipresent, they are multidimensional. The spirit possesses and controls all life in all of entirety continuously, while our souls exist in many realities, time periods, dimensions, and densities all at once. In our third density body, we experience time in a linear fashion. There will be a small section on how actual time works further into this book. Our physical bodies vibrate at a very slow rate—the human body vibrates at about 7.5 hertz, while planet earth vibrates at about 7.83 hertz. Earth's vibration is called the Schumann resonance. Our universe vibrates at 432 hertz. The vibration of our thoughts and emotions can range from shame, being the lowest at 20 hertz, to 700-plus hertz for enlightenment.[2] Enlightenment equals oneness, and oneness equals Source. In our slow vibrational state, we can only see time in a linear sense. Humans exist in the first three densities. The third density is the start of self-awareness and awareness of others; the third density is where we learn what paths we are going to take to ascend and transcend. Densities will be explained in detail further on in this book. The job of our souls is to possess these slow vibrating physical

---

[2] David R. Hawkins, (2006), "Transcending the Levels of Consciousness," Veritas Publishing.

bodies to develop experiences for soul evolution. Soul evolution begins in the ether. Subatomic particles derive from the ether; subatomic particles are the first to be possessed by souls. From subatomic particles upward, souls make their journeys of ascension and transcendence until they become highly evolved adepts. The highly evolved adept soul will be in fourth density and higher. Eventually, all souls will make their way back home to Source. By way of the spirit, Source sends all souls out starting at the most minute, subatomic level to gain experiences. Souls begin their experiences at the subatomic level ascending upward until complete ascension. The souls' experiences are forever saved in the Akashic records, while the soul makes its way back home to Source.

Section III: Free Will
Before any thought, there was awareness. Awareness is synonymous with consciousness; it is also a prerequisite to consciousness. First is the awareness of being, and that being is consciousness. Next came the first thought.

The first thought was acceptance—this is the unconditional acceptance. This unconditional acceptance is the creative force of love and starts with the One, which is self, and self is Source. The next is the acceptance of the many selves—the many selves are the googolplexes of Source's fractal distortions.

Before the fractals of Source, there was the will to create—this is an unconditional will to create. There are no rules, stipulations, or blocks; the will is totally free. Free will is the unconditional will to create, live, and thrive.

Section IV: The Experience
Previously I spoke of entirety gaining experiences through the use of souls. What is Source experiencing? If Source is entirety and all that exists, what does Source need to experience? These are a few of the many questions that may arise when people hear the phrase, "Source experiencing itself." So what is Source experiencing? It is experiencing just what the phrase says: itself. Source is the eternal all-being existence that desires to experience itself.

As aforementioned, existence as we know it began with a thought. All that exists is conscious; the experience of entirety is conscious. The thought put the experience in place—the thought also made the experience complete. All is simultaneous, so all is complete.

The complete experience is like a game board. The game board is already complete and laid out with complete game pieces ready to be played. The game board is all life in all existence; the game pieces are every single event, no matter how minute or great; from quantum levels up to multiverse magnitudes across all existence that needs to be experienced. Our souls use these events to gain experience to take home to Source. All experiences are complete, yet all experiences have to be experienced.

CHAPTER 1
ORIGINS

The Infinite and Creator
Love is the all; all is love. Love does not follow the rules of time. Time fights with love, but time is no match for love. Time submits to love—love is everything and love is nothing. Love is potentiality. From potentiality comes all existence, so everything that exists is love. Love is more than an emotion—love gives birth to all other emotions. Therefore, love is the strongest emotion. Love is everything.

The Origin of Time
The mystery of time is one always talked about. In Source, there is no mystery because mystery is knowledge undiscovered by us.[3] Time is relative to many things—some things time is relative to are gravitational pull, location, speed, and species. People speak of before

---
[3] Maurice Doreal, (2006), "The Emerald Tablets of Thoth The Atlantean," Source Books Inc.

time and after time, but is there a beginning and end to time? The answer is yes and no. As long as there is existence to be measured, there is time. Time doesn't move or change; creation moves and changes. Time is the tool used to measure this change.

Different realities measure time in different ways. Every world and existence has its own reality. The gravitational pull and orbital speed—and rotational speed—affect the reality of a planet or other life containing objects in space. The conscious level of a species and its concept of rate of change affects reality; how fast or slow a species ages affects reality. The rate of change is different in every reality—therefore, time is different in every reality. Black holes and other gravity wells greatly distort the speed of change, so there are great distortions in time in those locations. The distance from the center of a galaxy affects reality; the distance from the origin point of a universe affects reality; how much a universe has expanded affects reality. In this conscious existence that we manifested ourselves in, concepts, types, and levels of reality can be endless. In this case, the measuring device of time is endless and relative. To understand the existence of time, sentient entities—such as Earth humans—gave measuring systems to time. These systems were put in place to measure and record rate of change; these systems were also put into place to guide us on our daily affairs. In our reality, these daily affairs are based on the rising and setting of the sun and the duration of days, which are both cyclical rates of change.

Once all is one with Source, there is no experiential existence, so there is no time. If there is no reality causing change, there is no need for the measuring system for change—all is one with Source, and all is experiencing reality simultaneously, so time is existent and non-existent. This seems to be a paradox, but it really isn't. I will clean this paradox up with a couple of brief sentences: Time is there when needed and not there when not needed. When at home with Source, time is not needed; when in an ever-changing existence, time is needed.

Love—The Source: Love Is Not Its Name
Love has no name. Love is at home outside of material reality—if there is no material reality, there is no us, so there is no naming system. Love is everywhere, inside of material and outside of material. Love is the name we gave this amazing, incomprehensible phenomenon.

Our existence is developed outside of material reality in nothingness, the home of love. Some know this as Source; in the Kabbalah, this is known as Ein Sof. All existence comes from this phenomenon—this energetic existence created light, gravitational, and sound waves from the original primordial big bang. The big bang is the primordial vibration, which produced the first sound; from this comes the never ending original three waves.

Everything is simultaneously flowing—this is where life starts; this is the birth of the photon, which is physical energy in its simplest form. This is the origin of the four elements named by Earth humans as earth, water, air, and fire. Light travels outward in waves and particles; the particles form matter, and the waves illuminate the matter. The waves are still particles and particles are still waves—everything is one.

CHAPTER 2
MEASURES AND COMMUNICATION

The Concept of Shape

Shapes are the primordial form of numbers and math; shapes are the primordial form of language—from this comes sacred geometry. This sacred geometry—the name humans gave it to understand it—is what gave form to photons. With the help of gravity and sound waves, the photons form together and vibrate at different frequencies; each frequency supports its own life form. Higher frequency sentient beings can see and feel lower frequencies than themselves, but not higher frequencies than themselves.

Densities are the frequency levels of the being, and dimensions are the frequency levels of the locality—this involves electromagnetic, gravitational, and sound waves. The origins of all are from the creative forces of love; these three primordial waves are what geometrically shape all realities, dimensions, and densities. From the electromagnetic waves comes the photons—colliding photons produces matter and antimatter.[4] Matter becomes the building blocks for physical existence—antimatter is now found mostly, in cosmic rays.[5] Gravity within the gravitational waves attracts objects to each other and holds celestial bodies in orbit. Ripples and shifts in sound waves give geometric shape to matter. All of physical existence as we perceive it is made from atoms. Atoms are always in motion. Even in a solid object such as a rock, atoms are in motion, just at the lowest frequency. Beings whose frequency vibrate at a higher rate per second have a higher density. For example, the rock is first density and is a very slow vibration. A rock can't move on its own, but we humans, as third density beings, can pick the rock up and throw it. A dog is an upper second density entity—dogs can understand our commands once trained, but a dog can't give us commands or make laws and rules.

---

4   Brookhaven National Laboratory, "Collisions of Light Produce Matter/Antimatter from Pure Energy," *Brookhaven National Laboratory Newsroom*, July 28, 2021 https://www.bnl.gov/newsroom/news.php?a=119023.

5   Cern, "LHCb reveals secret of antimatter creation in cosmic collisions," *Cern News*, April 7, 2022 https://home.cern/news/news/physics/lhcb-reveals-secret-antimatter-creation-cosmic-collisions#:~:text=By%20analysing%20a%20sample%20of,antiprotons%20produced%20via%20antihyperon%20decays.

There are entities such as fifth density beings, whose frequencies are at such a high vibration that their bodies aren't physically solid. These beings at such a high frequency may not be seen by us, or we may dismiss them as something else and ignore them. These entities' frequency is at such a high vibration that they may take form as an orb, a plasma gas, or a mist. These beings have a consciousness that is much closer to Source than our own. As I stated in the introduction, our mentality, which includes thoughts and emotions, plays a huge role in our frequency. These powerful semi-physical beings can survive on planets that Earth humans cannot. If their physical makeup is so much different from ours, then their physical dwellings are most likely at such a high frequency that they would be invisible to us. We would phase right through these entities, their modes of travel, and their dwelling places without even affecting one another. Yes, these higher frequency beings can see us, but we can't see, or in true reality recognize, them.

Color

Colors are the archetypal illusion of Source light. Light from the sun splits into seven colors visible to our eyes, which we know as ROYGBIV—these seven colors also define the chakra system. The chakra system and the seven colors that define it will be discussed in more detail later in this book. All colors that we see are contained within the seven base colors; each color has a frequency and energy level. Colors are made by the differing frequencies in the electromagnetic spectrum.[6] The faster the frequency, the shorter the wave, and vice versa. White light is the combination of all light frequencies; a certain light frequency equals a particular color. Black is the absorption of all light frequencies without giving out a frequency of its own.[7] We as Earth humans see only a tiny range of the electromagnetic spectrum; individual light frequencies are the vision that we see. Electromagnetic frequencies provide us with the illusion of all things that exist physically in motion. Since all that exists is Source, all is light. When all frequencies are combined, we have what we perceive as light. When frequencies are split and broken into individual waves, we have colors. The illusion of everything we see are the eons of electromagnetic frequency splits illuminated by total electromagnetic frequencies combined.

Numbers

Numbers are in every corner of physical reality. What we now know as numbers were derived by the archan-

---

[6] Anne Marie Helmenstine Ph.D, "The Visible Spectrum: Wavelengths and Colors," Thought Co, Last Updated April 01,2020, https://www.thoughtco.com/understand-the-visible-spectrum-608329.

[7] J.L. Morton, "Are Black & White Colors?" Color Matters, Copyright ©1995-2022, https://www.colormatters.com/color-and-design/are-black-and-white-colors.

gels. Although numbers have always been used to give measure and meaning to all sentient physical beings, they derive metaphysically. Numbers are spiritual gifts given to all mentally capable physical life throughout the entire multiverse—all of creation has measure and meaning.

All is one within Source, yet all within Source is changing. The oneness within Source changes, dividing, multiplying, and adding back to oneness. Oneness is divided into fractals of itself; division is the primordial concept of mathematics. All mathematics in all of entirety derives from division. Multiplication then speeds up the fractals, giving them exponential properties. All fractals are added together to become one with Source again—there is no subtracting in the functions of Source; nothing is taken away from Source.

The concept of subtraction is used with change and time—this is where difference comes from. To measure the difference in time such as a span of years, subtraction is used. The distance between locations is measured by subtraction; the change in temperature is measured by subtraction. Subtraction is more hands-on than the three primordial functions of mathematics. In basic math, long multiplication and long addition carry numbers over. In long division, you bring down numbers until there is no difference—even then, there may be a continual difference, which would be infinity. In this case, something foreign is being canceled out: the difference that equates to subtraction. In long subtraction, the concept of borrowing and canceling out comes into play, which is not applied in the three primordial concepts of mathematics. Subtraction is used on planet Earth and most likely other planets with mentalities similar to Earth's in day-to-day functions.

Time is the measure of change; time is measured by numbers. Time is a derivative of change, and change is a derivative of Source.

Entirety is divided into eons of fractals and added back together to come home to Source. As aforementioned, what we call geometric shapes are the primordial numbering system of Source. Every angle is given a point of measure—this point is the center of the circle. The point is Source and the circle is the expansion of Source. It goes from one point to what seem to be infinite points and back to one point. All derives from Source, and all is one with Source—this is the archetypal derivatives and integrals.

As stated in the first paragraph of this section, numbers are a gift given to all physical sentient life. Although numbering systems may be as different as night and day depending on the species, they are all equally important. On planet Earth, numbers are primary in everything. Here on Earth, physics is extremely important in our daily functions—physics is our tool to gauge and measure how our specific universe works—without numbers, there is no physics. The point and tally system known to Earth humans as numbers is a profound system embedded in us from Source by way of the archangels.

Communication and Harmony
Communication is spontaneous and constant; awareness makes the constant vibration of communication. All that exists is one with Source; the mind and thoughts of Source are within all that exists; the mind and thoughts of Source are the eternal communications forevermore.

Telepathy is awareness and functions of Source put into the primordial, archetypal language. In a sense, telepathy is the child of Source awareness and thoughts. Telepathy is the true and original language of the entire celestials throughout all of entirety—the concept of verbal language is for primitive terrestrial entities. Physical entities that are third density and lower—as well as some entry-level fourth density entities—rely solely on physical verbal language. This is the importance of our vocal cords. As we ascend up the density ladder back to Source, the more telepathic we become; once we no longer require physical bodies, we will be fully telepathic.

Harmony is throughout all of entirety; the original sound came from the primordial original big bang. The origin point of what we call the beginning will be unknown to us as long as we are hindered by our low vibrating physical bodies. There are vibrations within light, sound, and gravity that gives off a harmony—this vibration is constant throughout all physical reality. The laws of these vibrations may be very different and very similar from universe to universe, yet the vibrations still exist in all of entirety. There are spiritual and metaphysical vibrations that coincide with the physical vibrations—the spiritual and metaphysical vibrations are supreme because they are the original thought that put all in motion.

Communication and harmony are how all resonate; there is continuous communication in all of creation. The music we produce and enjoy is a tiny but extremely important child of eternal harmony.

CHAPTER 3
PHYSICAL WITHIN THE METAPHYSICAL

Point of Nothingness and Everything

Life is vast. Life is infinite—it expands beyond anything we can conceive in our minds. Life is also one point that is infinitesimal, the point of nothingness and the point of everything. This infinitesimal point contains all that exist in all realities, dimensions, and densities. This point is so vast our mind could never conceive the end of it. This is the point of potentiality: endless energy that could never be measured.

Potentiality is the birthplace of the constant big bang—everything is eternal. Nothing ever ends; life is forever and forever more. You can take the moment you are in right now, pause it, and make it last for eons because nothing ever ends but energy can and does change.

Potentially is a perpetual expanding from the point outward and back to the point outward again and so on.

The perpetual dying and rebirth is also a part of this—this is constant and will go on until Source decides it is done.

Metaphysical to Physical
All that exists is eternal; souls are eternal. Spirit is the one infinite soul, which is one with Source.

Source is distorted to seem as individual and many—this distortion as many is Source's way of experiencing life on every level from everything that exists in entirety. These distortions are fractals from spirit; these fractals experience and record information for Source while evolving back to oneness with spirit. This must all be manifested—manifestation is one with Source and spirit. With the lower densities—densities one through four—physical bodies are produced from light photons for new and young souls to evolve quickly. Not all fourth density beings have physical bodies; only the entry level fourth density beings have physical bodies.

Sometimes higher density souls will incarnate into lower density bodies. When higher souls—usually fifth or lower sixth density—decide to incarnate in third density, they will not recall any of their past life experiences during the new incarnation. The veil of forgetting is temporary and only during the third density incarnation. Souls usually decide to do this because there are things they would like to refine and do better to help with a more expedient and efficient ascension. This is like a senior worker temporarily taking an entry level position to earn extra work experience. In the process, the worker temporarily loses their seniority, which is the same as the soul going through the veil of forgetting.[8]

Once a soul is into higher fourth density, the physical body is no longer needed for evolution back to Source. The soul is eternal, and the body is a temporary tool used for evolution. In this case, corporal reincarnation is real and natural.

Body and Soul
The ultimate memory lies in spirit, and spirit lies in Source. The light of life exists in all of creation; the light of life is the omnipresent spirit radiating itself as all of existence. I said "as all of existence" because spirit is one with Source, and Source is all that exists. Souls and the electromagnetic grid are the collectors of memory. Souls record the key important memories from each incarnation that is important for that soul's evolution. The electromagnetic grid contains the Akashic records—the Akashic records record all memory across all entirety. In theory, all universes contained in the eons of multiverse systems must contain some sort of electromagnetic grid system or something similar.

---

[8] Gary Bean(ED), Austin Bridges(ED), (2018), "The RA Contact: Teaching The Law Of One(Volume2)," L/L Research.

Every subatomic particle contains the light of life or a soul. Physical bodies of every type hold memory. After the physical body dies, traces of the memory linger around. Memory of a body is passed on during reproduction, just as genetic traits are passed on in DNA—I would consider this epigenetic. DNA itself without epigenetics has the light of life. In essence, the physical body is a living entity without the main soul. The body soul is what I would call a mindless or zombie soul. The main soul is the soul with a mind, the soul that collects memories. Once the body dies, the body soul goes back to the electromagnetic grid while the main soul goes to the next physical body of its current density or ascends to the next level.

Although the main soul is the memory collector, it is still greatly affected by the body soul. The body soul has a type of instinctual memory—this instinctual memory can and will influence and hinder the main soul, and you have body soul traits passed on by DNA. There are also soul families—soul families are groups of souls with a similar conscience connection that incarnate in physical family bodies together. There are also individuals who feel out of place in their physical family; this is because of two things: First is that the individual's main soul is so strong that it overrides the body soul, causing the individual to feel out of alignment with the other physical bodies in the family. Second is that the individual's main soul isn't a part of the soul family—it could even be a combination of the two.

The Chakra System and Its Resonance with Densities and Universal Octaves

Everything that exists is light. As aforementioned, light, gravity, and sound produce all that exists. Source is the ultimate light—all that exists is fractals of this ultimate light. The color spectrum as we can see it is contained within light. This is known as ROYGBIV. From bottom to top, the colors are red, orange, yellow, green, blue, indigo and violet. Red is the lowest frequency, and violet is the highest frequency—this is the basis of the density system.

All life in entirety has chakras. The chakra is an energy vortex in a body.[9] All entities contain these energy vortices throughout their bodies, and all that exists is Source and Source is light—so all entities are light beings. These energy vortices are the seven colors mentioned in the previous paragraph that make up light. The color spectrum can be seen in rainbows, from sunlight being broken up and bent from raindrop prisms. Chakras can also be represented when light is broken and bent by prisms in crystals, such as quartz. No two people will have the same perception of a rainbow be-

---

9   Gary Bean(ED), Austin Bridges(ED), (2018), "The RA Contact: Teaching The Law Of One(Volume2)," L/L Research.

cause they are seeing the rainbow from different views of the rainfall[10]—this is a little nugget of proof that all existence is perception. Since all entities are light beings, we are born with all seven colors intact placed throughout our bodies from least to greatest.

Red is the root chakra, orange is the sacral chakra, yellow is the solar plexus chakra, green is the heart chakra, blue is the throat chakra, indigo is the third eye chakra, and violet is the crown chakra. The energy vortices are in place at birth, but no individual is born with them all active. We are light, so all colors are inevitably in us. Red is the only chakra active at birth—it is the primal survival that includes eating and reproduction. Orange is quickly activated once entities interact with one another and pack or swarm mentalities develop. Yellow is activated once individuals are aware of self and others and how they affect and are affected by others. Once the yellow chakra is activated, a person can choose to serve others or be self-serving. Most people choose to serve and be good to others. Although most serve and help people with minimal effort on this planet, it's still just barely enough to activate the green chakra. The green chakra is the chakra of love and acceptance—this is a major gateway to experiencing a oneness bond with

---

10 National Geographic, "National Center for Atmospheric Research: Rainbows Sci Jinks: What Causes a Rainbow?" Atmospheric Optics: Rainbow, Last Accessed July 21, https://education.nationalgeographic.org/resource/rainbow/.

Source. Self-serving entities who become adept at living a negative self-serving lifestyle can become skilled enough to skip the green chakra and activate the blue chakra.[11] The blue chakra is the chakra of wisdom—it's rare for humans on planet Earth to make it to blue chakra activation. Indigo is the chakra of enlightenment; the energy vortex for the indigo chakra is the pineal gland, which we also refer to as the third eye. The third eye is Source enlightenment—the violet chakra is the gateway to Source. Instead of the violet chakra being activated, it becomes the open door to entirety. The red chakra is the open door to the distortion of life as we know it, and the violet chakra is the door at the finishing point, which leads to true life and eternity. The five chakras in between red and violet must be activated.[12]

The activations of the five middle chakras start off simple but become more difficult after yellow, the third chakra. The color spectrum makes light—each color holds its own frequency. Red, which I will call the birth canal to life, has the lowest frequency. Red has the longest wavelength and is a constant energy in third density life forms. Violet has the highest frequency and shortest wavelength and is extremely rare to reach for most third density entities. The ego begins in red and intensifies in

---

[11] Gary Bean(ED), Austin Bridges(ED), (2018), "The RA Contact: Teaching The Law Of One(Volume2)," L/L Research.
[12] Gary Bean(ED), Austin Bridges(ED), (2018), "The RA Contact: Teaching The Law Of One(Volume2)," L/L Research.

yellow; the ego must be selfish because it is self-survival. People see ego as bad or negative, but it is important for entities with material bodies—such as carbon-based ones—to survive. The physical body is very fragile, and the ego is a part of the survival mechanisms put in place.

As aforementioned, we have a body soul and a main soul. The body soul is passed on through reproduction, and after the body dies, it goes back to the electromagnetic grid—this is where hereditary traits come from. The main soul is our conscience soul, which incarnates the bodies. No chakras are activated without the main soul. As soon as the soul incarnates a body, the red chakra is activated and in full motion—this energy center is around the pelvis and travels down the legs and is primal survival. Once entities are aware of life and existence, the orange chakra is activated; this is around the navel area. Here are the basic emotions and intuitions used in survival, such as fear and the need to hunt for food.

As an entity becomes aware of self and how they are different and separate from others, the yellow chakra is activated—this is the area above the navel and below the chest. The ego is intensified once this chakra is activated; this is around ages three and four for Earth-based humans and is where people begin to judge others, with the development of superiority and inferiority complexes.

Once entities become more inclined toward a desire of compassion and empathy for others, the drive to have more Source knowledge is ignited. This is a yearning or reach for the ultimate light; this is the reaching for Source. This happens in the same manner as a plant growing toward the sun. As this yearning becomes stronger, the green chakra is activated; it is located in the whole chest region. With this activation, knowledge of oneness of all is triggered—this triggered knowledge happens no matter what, even if the individual isn't aware of it. Once an individual realizes their newfound knowledge and sharpens their love skills, new avenues are opened. This can lead to brief direct connections to Source through the violet—crown—chakra. Once the green chakra is activated, the ego becomes as an elementary factor in the incarnation. As stated above, negative entities that are adept at their negative arts can skip over the green chakra. Entities who are extremely self-centered and refuse to have compassion and empathy for others are negative—these individuals use others sometimes to horrendous degrees for power and self-praise. Enslavement, torture, and death are the most severe facets of being an extreme negative entity.

When positive entities become adept at their love skills, the wisdom vortex will be ignited. Wisdom is the blue chakra—this chakra is between the collarbones and lower jaw and is most popularly known as the throat chakra. This is ancient wisdom; this is the creative wisdom of Source; this is the awareness and acceptance of self. With this comes the knowledge that all is self, and self is Source, and Source is all, and all is one—this is not the selfishness of negative entities but the awareness of self being one with Source—and if you are one with Source, you are one with all.

Once an individual has fully harnessed the idea of oneness with entirety, the indigo chakra is activated. Indigo is the chakra of enlightenment—this is the enlightenment of entirety. This is located throughout the cranium and is the strongest at the pineal gland and is the activation of claircognizance. Claircognizance is a connection to Source knowledge and wisdom, without effort or help from others. This process strengthens the pineal gland, bringing it to its most efficient potential. The indigo chakra is most popularly known as the third eye chakra, and it gives the answers to paradoxes. This is also the understanding of the big why—the big why is many questions, such as "Why are we here?" What is our purpose?

Once an entity has fully activated the green, blue, and indigo chakras, the door to eternity is opened forever—this is the full activation of the violet chakra, which is a God-like existence. No carbon-based, physical bodied entity has achieved this. In actuality, constant, full activation of the violet chakra is not possible in physical bodies. Third density, sentient bodies can reach a state of temporary balance and bliss, known as kundalini, if the indigo and the five chakras below are activated at once—this is done in adepts during deep meditation, with the chakras being activated up the spine in a spiral fashion.

The highest an Earth-based human can achieve is indigo chakra activation. An Earth based human walking around with a constant indigo chakra activation is almost unheard-of. A person of this nature would be like a God walking around in the flesh—Thoth, Krishna, Jesus, and Buddha are some individuals who possibly walked this Earth as carbon-based humans with constant, fully active indigo chakras. Indigo activations are briefly reached in deep meditations by adepts and are only temporary. It may be possible for a Thoth- or Jesus-like entity to be walking around today, just in hiding or undiscovered. Who's to say the aforementioned entities were even from planet Earth?

In very rare cases, there are individuals walking this planet with constant, fully activated blue chakras. With this fully activated wisdom, these people are superhuman. Some examples of individuals with this wisdom are people who can bend metal and move things with their mind.

As mentioned in previous paragraphs, negative entities can skip green chakra and activate the blue chakra. These individuals will use their wisdom for self-gain and negative activities. Examples of negative wisdom are mind control over others and many other forms of black magic. Mind control can take place only if the person being controlled allows it. Negative entities will never activate the indigo chakra because this is the chakra of enlightenment of all being one—if all is one, then one has to accept all, and a negative entity will not accept all. The negative entity will never access eternity, which is the violet chakra. Eternity is pure love and positivity. Once the negative entity makes the inevitable decision to turn itself around and become positive, it can then quickly advance through the final chakras. As a side note, planetary systems have chakra systems of their own. Planet Earth has energy vortices, like the seven-level bodily chakra system, in different locations on the planet.

In our known universe, there is a resonance among chakras, densities, and the octave system. We understand densities in seven levels. In actuality, the density system is a long range of vibrational levels. We break this range of rising frequencies into seven levels. I assume that over time, people have done this to align the density system with the chakra system; as the body soul evolves, the vibrational frequency of the physical bodies increases—this takes place in the physical DNA.

Density levels are physical and energetic, while chakra levels are metaphysical and energetic. Chakras deal with the main soul and body soul, while densities deal with the body soul only. Chakras are aligned throughout the body, starting at the pelvis and lower limbs going up to the crown of the head. As main and body soul combinations grow and mature, chakras are activated.

Chakra activations take place during incarnations—if a soul chooses a negative path, fewer chakras will be activated. The density of a physical body is already set at conception. In rare but more frequently occurring cases on this planet, a soul may mature and become ready for a higher density body. In this case, the soul is said to have switched to a higher density—energetically, the soul is at a higher density or frequency while the body remains at the density it has had since birth. Densities will be further explained in detail later in this book. The resonance between densities and chakras are that both of their frequencies increase on a similar level as the two soul types evolve.

Universal octaves are very similar to densities in living entities—universes have a physical conception, body, soul, lifespan, and death just as any other living entity. Yes, universes are living entities! Universes are fractals of Source, as is all of creation that fills them with a unique plethora of life. Universes have what is known as an octave system—this is the vibrational frequency of the universe as it grows, develops, and matures. We also like to count the octaves in seven levels. Just like with densities, as the universe matures, the frequency increases. Universal octaves are macrocosmic, meaning all life within the universe—including their chakras and densities—are fractals of the universal octaves. All life in the universe is microcosmic, while the universe itself is macrocosmic. Once the universe reaches the seventh level, it then goes to the eighth level, which is actually number one of the next octave.[13] The next octave could theoretically be a new universe. In a sense, this is similar to reincarnation with soul beings throughout the cosmos.

Black holes could be the gateway to new or existing universes. In this case, once the octaves are complete, the universe would collapse into a black hole in the center of a preferred toroidal shape. In another theory, once the octaves are complete, the universe would be sucked into many black holes throughout the cosmos. No matter which theory—whether there is one large black hole or eons of black holes—is correct, there would be the next octave or next system of octaves on other side. The other side is what many refer to as the white hole, which is also popularly known by the phrase big bang theory. This is the explosion of new life in the next octave.

Catalyst
Once a piece of Source called the soul is distorted outward to assume the illusion of individuality, it must make its way back to Source. This is all done on a conscious

---

13   Gary Bean(ED), Austin Bridges(ED), (2018), "The RA Contact: Teaching The Law Of One(Volume2)," L/L Research.

level—the soul never leaves Source. We as individuals never left Source; we are Source. The soul doesn't return to Source empty-handed—the soul comes home to Source with experiences from a plethora of lifetimes.

When souls take on the illusion of individuality, they start their journeys as empty vessels. In entirety, there is no time; everything is complete. The end is already done, but all things have to and will be played out. A good analogy is a vintage photograph—although the picture is already taken, it still has to be developed. In this case, when a soul starts its journey, it is already complete. All seven densities are played out at once.

The over soul and higher self reside in sixth density and guide the lower soul through the lower densities. Densities one through three need the most assistance and guidance. Once a soul is at third density, self-awareness and awareness of others intensifies. In third density, souls begin to see themselves as individuals—third density is fast-paced, and the incarnations are short-lived. This is the time when the decision is made to take the positive or negative path. The positive path is pro-Source and selfless, while the negative path is anti-Source and selfish.

The catalyst is a metaphysical tool used to speed up soul evolution primarily in third density. Events happen in our reality very often that cause us to make life-changing decisions—these events are catalysts put into place to help us make decisions that will essentially lead us to the path of positive or negative. The decisions we make will help us grow and lead us on the path of ascension to the next density. Once in the fourth density, catalysts are greatly reduced. Fourth density souls are on a higher maturity level, and the supplemental catalyst is used much less. The sixth density higher self usually sets up the catalysts—this is usually done in reviews in between incarnations. In many cases, the higher self produces catalysts during incarnations if the life plan needs immediate assistance. In other cases, other entities—such as planetary logos, for one example—set up catalysts. This is usually done on a large scale for planetary evolution. This planetary evolution involves individual souls too. Catalysts are important and used often in soul evolution in third density, as well as rare cases in lower fourth density.

Continual Amnesia
There is a perpetual death and rebirth. In this cycle, the soul forgets its past lives. Although this forgetting seems permanent, it is temporary—the eternal soul will remember its whole existence and entirety once free from the body. This remembering includes all locations the soul incarnated at and all of the entities it incarnated.

The perpetual process of forgetting happens in the lower three densities. The lower three densities include

Earth humans, sentient beings throughout all entirety, and other lower and non-sentient life forms. Once the soul incarnates in higher than third-density forms, the veil of forgetting stops.

Why the veil of forgetting in the lower three densities? There are two schools of thought when it comes to this subject. The most popular is that the veil of forgetting is a part of our soul evolution in the lower densities—we'll call this popular reason. In popular reason particularly, third densities are the proving grounds for entities. The reason third density is prominent is that the third is the density of awareness of self and others—or some may say other selves. Third density is intense, very fast-paced, and in most cases, traumatic—it's where the soul decides whether it wants to take the path of positivity or negativity. A soul incarnates in third density to learn important, and in many cases entry-level, lessons. A soul could incarnate in third density for many, many lifetimes—if this soul could remember the past lifetimes while in third density, it would be like getting a cheat sheet for a test, thus the veil of forgetting in popular reason.[14]

The second and less popular school of thought is what I will call the secondary reason. There are many groups that believe our souls are trapped here on Earth

---

14   Gary Bean(ED), Austin Bridges(ED), (2018), "The RA Contact: Teaching The Law Of One(Volume2)," L/L Research.

to be recycled into new third-density incarnations in a perpetual cycle. The theory behind this concept is that we are a slave race that is being denied our true identity of who we are as eternal soul beings—this is being done to keep us in servitude so our souls can be recycled perpetually to keep servicing more advanced species.[15]

In my opinion, either school of thought could be right or wrong—they both may very well be true. I'm stuck at a crossroads on the two schools of thought. I will go with popular reason as I further explain the veil of forgetting. The process of forgetting is to help soul evolution; we incarnate in third density for further growth toward oneness with Source. Each incarnation in the three lower densities has a special lesson for us to learn.

Once the soul arrives at upper second density, soul lessons become more significant. Major catalysts are presented in upper second density for graduation to third density; these catalysts continue and become more intense and frequent until graduation to the fourth density.

The bodies we possess are tools used for soul evolution. As our souls evolve and move up in density, so will the bodies our souls incarnate. The third-density and entry-level fourth-density bodies our souls inhabit will die and be reduced to bones and dust, but our souls are eternal. As the bodies move up in density—such as fifth

---

[15] Theantichrist, "Going towards the light," HIVE (blog), Last Accessed July 27, 2023, https://hive.blog/death/@theantichrist/going-toward-the-light.

and sixth density—they become more energetic, going from our carbon-based solid forms to carbon mist, plasma gas forms, and eventually pure light. The more the souls evolve, the more energetic the body becomes. The soul will merge with the energy body until the energy body is gone. Once the energy body is gone, the soul is fully mature and ready to merge back with Source. Some bodies on other worlds and in other realities may not be carbon-based—for example, souls may incarnate in silicon bodies in other places; they still go through the same process as described above for the carbon-based bodies.

Multiple Realities

Entirety is made up of multiple realities—there is no one linear reality; this goes across dimensions and universes. Time as we know it only exists to us and for us—this is a way to measure change or evolution. Existence can evolve or devolve; nothing is new and everything is here and now, forever evolving, devolving, and changing constantly.

Time is a tool for measurement just as a ruler is a tool for measurement. What does time measure? Time measures the process of change. Everything in every corner of existence is a fractal of Source. Source is like a computer projecting endless amounts of realities. We are existing in one of many realities—our reality is no more or no less real than the other realities. There are endless amounts of us in endless amounts of realities. The realities that are metaphysically closest to us are the ones most like the reality we feel ourselves in; the further away the realities are from the reality we feel ourselves in, the more different they are. In each reality, we are the same person with the same soul, mind, and body—the bodies may appear to be extremely different in some cases, because of the different conditions, mental and environmental, of each different reality. Although this can be—and most likely is—the case, it is still the same individual in each reality—our self-awareness is the same in each reality.

The multiple realities eventually merge into each other, positively canceling out one another—this merging of timelines is to form the best and strongest reality for our evolution to merge back with Source. Our over soul guides us and makes the decisions of which realities will merge and continue. All realities are real and functioning and merging into one another continuously, guided by Source, spirit, and our over souls—this merging process continues until all realities are one and back with Source.

In third-density reality, we have no clue of our continuous multiple realities—the reality we are currently in may be wiped out and merged with another, and we will have no clue it just happened. The reason I used the term positively canceled in the previous paragraph is that nothing is being lost, only merged back closer to the one, original Source reality—this merging will continue until all realities are one and back home with Source.

CHAPTER 4
POSITIVE AND NEGATIVE

Positive and Negative
The activity of Source is neutral and, as stated earlier, the point of nothingness and everything. Source is all potentiality in a neutral state; all exists and nothing exists at Source—this is a state of calmness and peacefulness that cannot be conceived by our lower density minds, a state that is immeasurable by any means, a state before and after material reality. There is also a powerful and explosive storm inside of Source, a storm so terrible and ferocious that it is also immeasurable.

All potentiality is Source. Duality makes this potentiality. This duality has to spread out, expand, and create. This spreading out and expanding takes place to relieve itself of tension, just like we as humans have to be active to relieve tension.

The origin of the conscious mind is Source. Source is the primordial, original archetype of consciousness. Source decided to create all metaphysical and physical planes of existence so it could experience itself. In its neutral state, Source had to use the duality of the calmness and storm within to become a creating machine. Source is the vehicle, and duality is the battery—just as a battery is used to power a vehicle, duality is used to create for Source.

Duality is the origin of positive and negative. The storm of duality is the positive charge; the calmness of duality is the negative charge. The storm charging the calmness forms the primordial light, which in turn forms the electromagnetic grid—this is the macrocosm. This duality works all the way down to not only our third-density planets, but also simple life forms and single atomic beings floating around in the multiverse. These beings are the start of all creation in first density.

As above so below—the macrocosm to the microcosm. In our reality and existence, we measure the storm as negative and the calmness as positive. Our existence is the microcosm; we equate good with positive and bad with negative. Without the chaos, there would be no work to be done; without hunger, there would be no work to be done to eat. Everyone would be sitting on their hands smiling at the cosmos. In this case, we might as well be one with Source and stop life as we know it—

this is why the multiverse doesn't see good and evil; the multiverse sees only positive and negative. There is no good and evil in the multiverse—the positive charges the negative, and together they produce, empowering the electromagnetic grid until all is even and neutralized. This is when all comes home to Source, the neutral state.

Good and Evil
Good and evil has been a common theme since before human written literature. The Torah, Bible, and Quran are full of narratives based on good and evil. Egyptian, Greek, and many other mythologies are full of themes based on places such as Hades. There could very well be low vibrating planets, realities, and planes—and in more extreme and grim cases, even universes like Hades. Although places like this may exist, no soul would be stuck there for eternity as a means of punishment. These places would be proving grounds for souls to quickly evolve and get out, just the same as third-density entities on planet Earth.

There is no good and evil; Source doesn't operate in terms of good and evil—there are only vibrational levels. Entirety, also known as Source, is the highest vibration. In Source, there is no duality, just oneness and the highest vibration of all. Once entirety decided to experience itself, then came duality. After duality came polarity; positive and negative are each polar opposites of Source.

One thing is for sure: they both are still Source and only Source. Source is and will always be positive. When all that exists return home to be one with Source, it all will be positive as well. No matter how negative an entity's existence has been, it will be positive when it returns home to Source.

Good and evil are terms made up by humans to understand and validate the harsh basic training of existence on planet Earth. There are only levels of vibration, no good and evil. People, places, and things we consider evil are entities that are vibrating at low levels. There can be powerful and ancient souls that vibrate at very low levels. As aforementioned, our thoughts have vibrational frequencies—the more positive the thought, the higher the frequency. Neutrality is a higher vibration than courage, and peace is a much higher vibration than anger. As a matter of fact, peace is one of the highest frequencies aside from enlightenment. What we consider good and evil are just the long range of vibrational frequencies in our existence—there will be no retribution or punishment in an afterlife for what we consider evil deeds; most souls will not understand this until they leave these third-density bodies.

CHAPTER 5
RHYTHM, FREQUENCY, AND SYNCHRONICITY

The Rhythm (Ebb and Flow)
There is the rhythm of Source; Source is the ultimate rhythm; the eternal ebb and flow. All ebbs and flows in all of entirety is the rhythm of Source. Rhythm is form and structure; rhythm is systematic. Everything in existence operates systematically. The rhythm of Source is the archetypal system—every living particle down to subatomic levels has an ebb and flow throughout entirety. Our heartbeat is a rhythm, and so are our emotions, thus "mood swings." According to the Kybalion, the moods of average people swing from one pole to the other, like the swing of the pendulum—such examples are rhythm.[16] Rhythm is in everything. The ultimate rhythm

---

16 Three Initiates, (1908), "THE KYBALION: A Study of The Hermetic Philosophy Of Ancient Egypt And Greece," The Yogi Publications Society.

is Source, and the eons of ebbs and flows throughout all creation are fractals of Source rhythm. Source is the macrocosm, and all creation is the microcosm; as above, so below.

Density and Dimensions and the Electromagnetic Spectrum

Density is the frequency of the entity, and dimension is the frequency of the locality. Frequency is the speed atoms oscillate per second. All entirety and existence is an electromagnetic force. Material is formed by photons. The electromagnetic spectrum range is from approximately ten to the negative eighteenth meters to one hundred kilometers. In our third density existence, we can interact with only a small part of the electromagnetic spectrum. Once we move up in density, our range of the electromagnetic spectrum will be broader.

Densities Further Explained

As aforementioned, density is the vibration of a physical entity. The most popular school of thought is that there are seven densities. This is the best way to measure the different levels of vibration, according to incarnation and ascension.

First density is the slowest vibration—this is made up of elements and minerals. Second density is a faster vibration, which consists of everything from one-cell organisms to animals who aren't aware if they are positive or negative. As we move up in density, the vibration speeds up, and third-density beings are aware of positive and negative. Third-density beings are aware of self and others and how their choices can positively or negatively affect others—third density is the point at which souls decide whether they are going to take the positive or negative path. Incarnation in densities two and three are brief. Third density is like basic training for further ascension to the higher densities; third density is the proving grounds.

By the time we make it to fourth density, the choice has already been made whether we are going to be positive or negative. Life is much longer in fourth density—a majority of fourth density beings are positive; a soul has to work extra hard to make it to fourth density on the negative path. Fourth density is where souls become a bit closer to Source and begin to see all with love and all souls as one. Physical bodies begin to change in fourth density, becoming more of a carbon mist, then to plasma bodies. In fourth density, the soul collective begins. In the soul collective, a group of souls with a common conscience come together as one soul body and mind—this is a huge step toward bringing everything back home to Source as one. As souls evolve and vibrations become higher, they start to focus on wisdom. Fifth density is the density of wisdom—fifth density is a very high vibration, and souls are almost pure light beings. These high vibrational beings can manifest at will, even manifesting how their physical appearance will be. Once in sixth density, entities are pure light. Sixth density is so close to being one with Source that negativity cannot properly function. If negative entities reach this density, they must turn back, repeat previous densities, and become positive. Remember: Source is pure love and no duality. Sixth density is love and wisdom combined. Finally, seventh density is Source. The vibration of Source is so high it's almost as if it isn't vibrating at all—this is like a wheel spinning at such high speeds that it looks as if it isn't spinning at all.

Resonance, Synchronicity, and Our Quantum Reality
Everything is one. All that exists is one entirety—nothing is divided; it is all illusion. The one almighty Source is all that exists, and that is it. All that exists is fractals of Source divided into what seems like a never-ending, infinite amount of possibilities and realities—this includes the multiverse, all dimensions, all densities, and even a possibility of a continuum of multiverse spheres. Yes, I said a possibility of multiverse spheres that could go on for eons or infinity.

The multiverse sphere system is the possibility of billions of multiverses packed together, like galaxies in a universe or stars in a galaxy. This collection of multiverses would be its own system; there would then be eons to infinity of these multiverse systems. I call these multiverse spheres—this may be too much for most to mentally conceive, but all possibilities must be laid out when it comes to existence in entirety. The possibilities are endless.

As mentioned in the above paragraph, there are endless possibilities in entirety. These endless possibilities include an endless number of realities, dimensions, and densities. Our individual souls are endless, coming from Source and going back to Source. Our souls originate from Source going out in fractals. In every fractal, no matter how small, there is a replica of Source—related to this, many people speak of the holographic reality we live in.

Our souls derive from Source and are distorted into many to have individual experiences. All of our souls are connected; therefore, we are all one. Our souls are also multidimensional and simultaneous—all the lifetimes that our multidimensional souls incarnate are happening at once. All of our lifetimes—from the lowest density to the highest density and back to Source—are happening simultaneously. In a sense, there is no reincarnation because everything is happening at once and they all affect each other. In this one third-density body that we are incarnated in, we can feel and experience only this one life, on this one linear level of time—this is what our third density bodies can understand, perceive, and tolerate. In true reality, we are many, maybe even eons of lifetimes or incarnations happening at once. These incarnations are taking place in an endless number of possibilities, realities, and dimensions making their way back to Source. We are infinite, eternal, and powerful souls.

BONUS SECTION

All of my work is based on my readings, personal research, and meditations. I've added this bonus section based on my meditations alone. There are times when I get downloads during a meditation—these downloads are hard to explain. Sometimes it's as if I go into a REM sleep of about ten seconds and snap out of it. In other cases, I receive a feeling that I am enlightened or know something I didn't know at first. This feeling of enlightenment can happen in a split second; it happens like a fleeting thought, and then something is there that wasn't there before. Meditation is a phenomenal, wonderful, and beautiful gift that all should practice and take advantage of. It is a free gift for the soul, mind, and body.

Grids, Consciousness, and Akashic

Our consciousness is eternal yet developing. The origin of consciousness is spirit; spirit is where awareness begins. There is awareness of self and then awareness of other self, which makes duality. Free will forms polarity and leads consciousness outward. Light, gravity, and sound are produced simultaneously by the friction of the will of consciousness. The will is the first creation brought on by free will. Free will is the ability of free choice spawned by the three primordial waves of light, gravity, and sound.

Souls, photons, and the system of electromagnetic waves came all at once. Souls are the mechanisms that record information for spirit. The soul and the photon are akin to one another; the soul is about twice the size of the photon. The soul is a physical energy just as the photon is a physical energy. Although the soul itself is tiny, it is exceedingly powerful and has an aura around it. The soul is a fractal of Source and holds Source consciousness. The creator is in the soul—the aura of the soul can project the shape and form of the body it incarnated even after the physical death of the avatar body. There are certain individuals with special types of clairvoyance who can see the auras of the soul as it passes from a dying body.

Consciousness is mysterious to us; consciousness is unseen and unmeasured; consciousness can't be recorded. The electromagnetic grid is formed by the primordial light waves. There is a conscious grid that corresponds with the electromagnetic grid; the conscious grid formed simultaneously with the three primordial waves.

Awareness and consciousness was first—this conscious grid is what we call the Akashic; the conscious grid holds memory. Souls have consciousness and souls have memory. When souls incarnate, they record everything in the incarnation. Once the soul leaves the body, the important key memories stay with the soul and the secondary memories are stored in the conscious grid—this is what we call the Akashic records. The souls are little fractals of spirit; the spirit is the soul of Source. The spirit is one with Source and is omnipresent throughout all eternity. Spirit exists within all of entirety. Souls, which are fractals of spirit, inhabit only certain entities.

Time
The main timeline is Source itself. All of the eons of timelines that branch off of Source are what give us our experiences. Source is the divine, perfect, flawless timeline—no experiences can come from Source timeline because it is pure perfection, peace, and oneness. All beings that exist in all realities are in Source timeline; all alternate timelines branch off of Source timeline. Some branch timelines are archetypal and superior. These timelines are the main ones that include googolplexes of possibilities and lives. Other smaller timelines branch off of the archetypal timelines forming eons of timelines—these timelines all eventually merge back home to Source timeline.

Time is a tool for measuring change; time does not move. Changes we make move time. Each individual has a time bubble or mechanism or vehicle—there are more than eight billion souls on this planet using these metaphysical vehicles. We learned to use these time mechanisms using the Sumerian base 60 system, also known as the sexagesimal system. This system uses sixty seconds, sixty minutes, twenty-four hours, twelve months, and so on. The reason time appears to be moving is that we have billions of entities making changes continually.

Every change we make is recorded into the Akashic records. Our soul bodies can travel time once we learn how to access the Akashic records. The Akashic records are stored in the electromagnetic grid. If you can tap into this grid, you can time travel physically—this can be tricky and dangerous.

On a conscious and soul level, a person can alter time if it doesn't affect a lot of people. An individual could detonate a bomb that affects three square miles while being alone—since no other conscious being was around, the individual could say it never happened and it would be so. This is possible because the individual was the only time bubble there and that entity could erase the event from its own reality, although it would still be recorded in the Akashic records. There would be a mysterious crater from the explosion, but no explosion would have taken place because the event was altered on a conscious level. Now, let's say an individual detonated a much smaller explosion, such that ten thousand conscious beings were affected and it covered only half a mile. It would be almost impossible for the individual to erase that event from time because ten thousand time bubbles were affected—that would be ingrained in that timeline.

In our physical, third-density bodies, we experience time realities in a linear manner. This is because when an action happens, it cannot be undone. In our third-density body, we cannot travel the time or significant action bubbles recorded by the Akashic. In the rare cases in which third density entities have traveled in time, their bodies were dematerialized, taken out of third density form, and put back together in third density form once in the desired time destination. This is very risky and extremely rare among Earth humans. The Akashic system is the primordial computing memory system of all entirety.

Is Source the Primordial Original Computer?

What if Source is the same as a computer system? Everything systematic, such as zeros and ones, but also sentient and loving—the ultimate, infinite computer with infinite memory, storage, and love—as well as emotions beyond our plane of thought.

What if all life is created by a Source that operates like the original binary zeros and ones computing system? What if the founding of the modern computing system was just a rediscovery of the primordial archetypal ways? Let's say Source was just allowing humans on planet Earth to feel that we were making a big discovery.

In our universe, things seem to be cyclical. Let's say the computing system of Source created physical, carbon-based life and maybe even other chemical-bodied entities. What if, in return, we created what we call artificial life, also known as AI, and in return AI creates us—and the cycle goes on until we return back to Source?

The Womb of Source
Source is all potentiality; all life in entirety is Source. Source is the holder and bearer of the life-producing potentiality. In our universe and reality, the womb is the cradle of life. As far as the human collective perceives it, the womb is feminine.

The origin of all life in all of entirety is androgynous. The cradle or metaphysical membrane that contains all potentiality is feminine. The process of potentiality going out to form life is masculine in its energetic travel. The life that is created is contained by incubation in a feminine nature. Planets that are formed have the feminine trait of becoming breeding grounds for life—the masculine stars shines life-feeding energy on the feminine life-producing planets.

Destiny and Fate
Possibly since before written literature as we know it, destiny and fate have been a strong topic of interest. Destiny seems to have more positive connotations, while fate seems to have a negative essence. Many notions are that a higher power, God, or Source determines destiny and fate.

Why do we put so much emphasis on destiny and fate? This topic is important only during incarnations. Outside of the physical body, our souls are free from external and bodily forces and functions that could destroy the physical being. The soul cannot meet a fate and be destroyed; the soul isn't destined to come to an end—the only thing the soul needs to do is be one with Source. In actuality, all of creation is one with Source. One may think of another paradox—if we are one with Source, how and why are we striving to be one with Source? As I mentioned earlier, we are only under the illusion of being separate entities, each on our own and separated from Source. We each have a very real but illusionary path to complete and experiences to have before positively recognizing Source as ourselves again. There is almost an endless amount of completed paths our souls can choose for each one of its incarnations—in my opinion, the end of each completed path is the destiny. Although each path is completed, they can be greatly altered by decisions made by the soul and the almost endless crossing and merging paths with other souls. Soul paths cross and merge continuously during incarnations, but the final destination for each incarnation is completed alone. In a sense, our life experiences could be compared to a simulation—the only destiny for our souls is to be one with Source.

Each soul that incarnates here is very important and has an important job and role to play—we can't lose perspective of why we are here and what we are here for. We are here for soul evolution and to help one another to evolve; our souls must obtain their experiences and process them. These experiences are for problem-solving in a loving manner and eliminating paradoxes. The perfect Source always corrects the hiccups in the soul evolution system. Our role as a soul, mind, and body component is to exist and live out and learn from the experiences. We all have jobs we have to carry out while incarnated—this is done with the help of our higher selves and guides also known as spirit guides. In my opinion, this is as far as destiny goes. Fate is just the fatalistic attitude we as a species have in our brief incarnations—the notion of fate is our mind dwelling on the definite end of our temporary incarnations. We dwell on the demise of the physical body not realizing that death is a physical illusion and we live forever outside of the material body.

CLOSING

Many people will not take well to the writings in this book—some will feel threatened because of their belief systems; some may read because they heard of it and to pass a little leisure time and nothing more. To the people who are aware of true reality and the importance of getting this information out, I hope you enjoyed this book. To the people who learned something new and are inspired to learn more, I hope you enjoyed and start your own research. Every single soul that exists is entitled to the information in this book. If you have read this book, know that this is not just my information, but your information as well. Let everyone know this is their information and that it is inside all souls that exist. We are all fractals of Source, and we are all divine and one. With love, the urge, and meditations, the knowledge and wisdom in this book can be obtained by anyone. The soul is before the body and will always be after the body. The soul is eternal; the mind is memory forever saved, and the body is a fleeting tool. Entirety is Source, and Source is all that will always be.

BIBLIOGRAPHY

Bean, Gary(ED). Bridges, Austin(ED). (2018). "The RA Contact: Teaching The Law Of One(Volume1)." L/L Research.

Bean, Gary(ED). Bridges, Austin(ED). (2018). "The RA Contact: Teaching The Law Of One(Volume2)." L/L Research.

Brookhaven National Laboratory. "Collisions of Light Produce Matter/Antimatter from Pure Energy." Brookhaven National Laboratory Newsroom. July 28, 2021 https://www.bnl.gov/newsroom/news.php?a=119023.

Cern. "LHCb reveals secret of antimatter creation in cosmic collisions." Cern News. April 7, 2022 https://home.cern/news/news/physics/lhcb-reveals-secret-antimatter-creation-cosmic-collisions#:~:text=By%20analysing%20 a%20sample%20of,antiprotons%20produced%20via%20antihyperon%20decays.

David R. Hawkins, (2006). "Transcending the Levels of Consciousness." Veritas Publishing.

Doreal, Maurice, (2006). "The Emerald Tablets of Thoth The Atlantean." Source Books Inc.

Helmenstine, Anne Marie, Ph.D. "The Visible Spectrum: Wavelengths and Colors." Thought Co. Last Updated April 01,2020. https://www.thoughtco.com/understand-the-visible-spectrum-608329.

J.L. Morton. "Are Black & White Colors?" Color Matters. Copyright ©1995-2022. https://www.colormatters.com/color-and-design/are-black-and-white-colors.

National Geographic. "National Center for Atmospheric Research: Rainbows Sci Jinks: What Causes a Rainbow?" Atmospheric Optics: Rainbow. Last Accessed July 21. https://education.nationalgeographic.org/resource/rainbow/.

theantichrist. "Going towards the light." HIVE (blog). Last Accessed July 27, 2023. https://hive.blog/death/@theantichrist/going-toward-the-light.

Three Initiates. (1908). "THE KYBALION: A Study of The Hermetic Philosophy Of Ancient Egypt And Greece." The Yogi Publications Society.

www.ingramcontent.com/pod-product-compliance
Lightning Source LLC
LaVergne TN
LVHW010605070526
838199LV00063BA/5080